FORKS

Twilight Territory

A Fan's Guide to Forks and LaPush

Forks Forum a Division of
Sound Publishing
19351 8th Avenue NE Suite 106
Poulsbo, WA 98370

Forks Forum
Post Office Box 300
494 South Forks Ave.
Forks WA 98331
www.forksforum.com
e-mail: editor@forksforum.com

Chris Cook - Sound Publishing

Twilight Territory Updated Edition A Fan's Guide to Forks and LaPush
ISBN 978-0-615-65244-3
June 2012

Forks Forum
Twilight Territory Updated Edition A Fan's Guide to Forks and LaPush
Text and Photos By Chris Cook, Editor Forks Forum

Printed in the United States of America

Decorative type set in Adobe Isabella
AND SPARTAN ONE TWO MONOTYPE

FORKS FORUM

Twilight Territory

Updated Edition

<><><><><><><><><><><><><><><><><><><><><><><><><><>

A Fan's Guide to Forks and LaPush

A Forks Forum Book
Forks, Washington

*Dedicated to the people of
Forks and LaPush,
to Twilight fans who visit Forks,
and to Twilight fans who,
for now,
only can dream of touring
the West End of the
Olympic Peninsula*

Twilight site direction sign located in front of
Twilight Central - Lepell's Flowers & Gifts.

CONTENTS

Forks Thriftway, where Bella Swan shops, lit up at night.

The entrance to Chinook Pharmacy in Forks, drawn by Forks artist Vern Hestand.

Welcome Twilight fans

Twilight Territory is an attempt to picture the Twilight phenomenon as manifested in the rural northwest Washington towns of Forks and LaPush, real places author Stephenie Meyer chose as the backdrop to her now globally-popular Twilight book series.

In *Twilight Territory*, we aim at providing for visting fans – and for fans who are reading this from the comfort of their homes – an authentic, informed fan's guide to the hometowns of Twilight written from the viewpoint of the West End's hometown newspaper, the *Forks Forum*.

This second edition of *Twilight Territory* provides an update on the Twilight locations and businesses of Forks and LaPush, and a look at Twilight happenings here since the first edition of *Twilight Territory* was published in 2009.

A steady stream of Twilight-focused articles and photographs appear in the pages of the weekly issue of the *Forks Forum*. This overview from within Twilight territory offers readers insights that take local knowledge and local access and time, something that visiting journalists are unable to capture in its entirety.

We also hope to provide a snapshot of the Twilight phenomenon for the residents of the West End, a look at how the global attention the community is receiving is coming to life daily with the arrival of Twilight fans.

The beginning of it all was simple.

The author began searching on Google.com for a rainy, dreary place to set her love story of reformed, ageless vampires, a police chief's daughter and youthful Native American werewolves.

Thanks to Fork's reputation as the rainiest town in the lower 48 states, what is known as the West End of the Olympic Peninsula became the backdrop of "Twilight," her first book in the series. Thanks to the Internet, the author was able to pick up background imagery initially without traveling to Forks and the West End.

Thanks to Stephenie Meyer's skill as a writer, Forks and the West End have taken on an alternate, fictionalized life in the pages of the Twilight books. Millions of readers now have their own vision of Forks. The misty rainforest, majestic Pacific coast and the rural logging town landscape are idealized in the minds of those enthralled by the love story of a newcomer Forks High School girl who falls for Forks and LaPush boys with deep secrets.

This has resulted in Forks and LaPush becoming the place Twilight fans just have to see. They drive out on Highway 101 from Seattle to the east or Portland to the south to this isolated Twilight world set in the dense Northwest coastal Douglas fir, hemlock and red cedar forest. The trip is seen as a pilgrimage of sorts for dedicated Twilight fans.

In the close-knit rural logging community of Forks, and along the coast at LaPush where the Native American Quileute Nation has existed for thousands of years, Twilight fans are easily spotted. A few years ago, seeing excited Twilight-focused visitors clutching digital cameras and shopping bags wandering the towns was a remarkable novelty.

Twilight Territory tells what there is to do and see here, with the basic information needed to find your way around, enhanced with in-depth, photo-rich descriptions. These include listings of Twilight-focused shopping, dining and accommodations available in Forks and LaPush and how to find your way to Forks from Seattle, the closest major airport to the West End; our own Twilight tour, which serves as an introduction for fans actually visiting, as well as a way for fans unable to make the journey to vicariously take the tour from home; a look at the early days of the Twilight phenomenon and the role we've played; an account of the annual Stephenie Meyer Day-Bella's Birthday celebration held on or about Sept. 13 each year; a special visit to LaPush, which includes a look at how the ancient traditions of the Quileute people tie in to "Team Jacob."

"Why wasn't the 'Twilight' movie filmed in Forks and LaPush?" is a question often asked of the Forks Forum by fans and local residents. We do regret that the feature film version of "Twilight" was filmed elsewhere, and we think filming at the actual location would have lent a touch of authenticity to the movie. Our response is a look at real locations and people we think should have been used in the film.

We hope *Twilight Territory* is a fun, informative guide that adds something special to the Twilight fan world. Watch for regular updates on Forks and LaPush Twilight news at the *Forks Forum* Web site at www.forksforum.com.

The Twilight Phenomenon and Forks

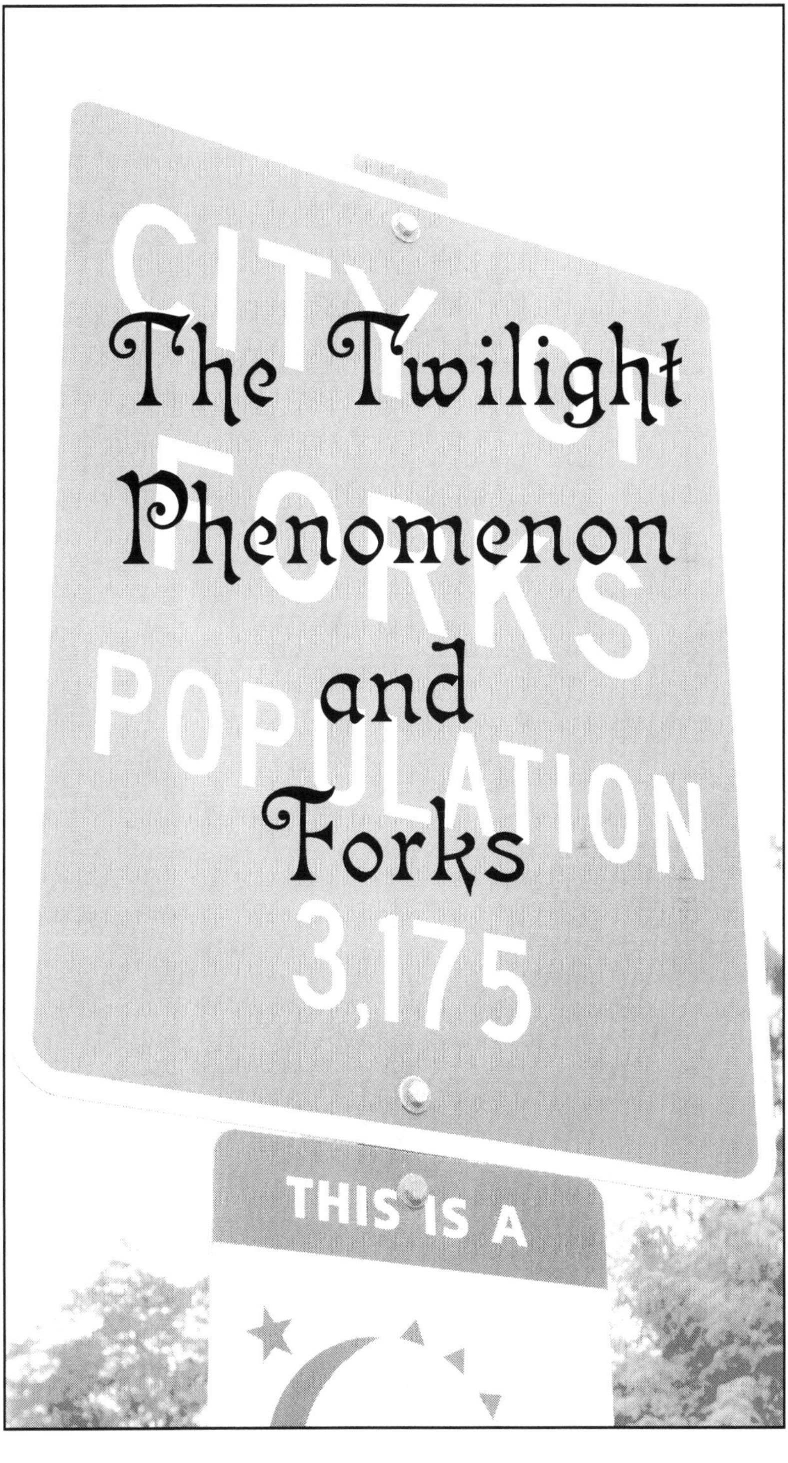

TwilightMoms.com group visits Forks, summer 2008.

Author Stephenie Meyer discovered Forks and nearby West End towns and settings during an Internet search she made while writing the first book in her Twilight series. She sought a rainy, misty, foggy place as the backdrop to her story of Edward, a handsome century-old high school student whose family members happen to be vampires, and his classmate and girlfriend, Bella.

Stephenie traveled with her sister Emily to Forks in 2004 after she began writing Twilight. In the Forks' section of her stephenie-meyer.com Web site she says she was afraid the actual town would be a disappointment, but instead "it was an incredible experience...it was eerily similar to my imaginings."

As the popularity of Stephenie's book grew following its release in October 2005, avid fans of Twilight began making regular visits to Forks, surprising local residents and businesses in the logging town with their knowledge of the area and their love of Twilight, the book's characters and of its setting.

Unlike the imaginary characters conjured up in Stephenie's imagination, Forks High School, Forks City Hall, Thriftway-Forks Outfitters, LaPush, First Beach, Forks Library and other locales in Twilight are real places, with the Twilight mentions adding a magic touch to the rural logging town. Visitors delight in completing their "pilgrimage" to Forks and the West End, finding a wide range of accommodations and unique souvenirs to take home.

Stephenie Meyer visited Forks again in July 2006 to be honored by the local community for the success of "Twilight," the first book in the author's Forks-set Twilight book series. Forks Mayor Nedra Reed declared July 20, 2006 Stephenie Meyer Day, and presented a proclamation to Stephenie, along with the distribution of garlic seeds to local residents. *Forks Forum* correspondent Carole Rose quoted Reed,

Westlands – model for the Cullen House?

A drive down a countryside road off Highway 101 east of Forks takes you to another world, an ideal Twilight location and the location of a home that may have inspired Twilight author Stephenie Meyer. When Meyer visited Forks in 2004 during the writing of Twilight, a large "historic home for sale" sign directed interested buyers and the curious to the home, which is known on the West End as Westlands. At the same time, detailed photographs of Westlands were posted on the Web site of Forks real estate firm Lunsford & Associates. There is speculation that the author either drove up to the house or possibly viewed it on the Lunsford & Associates Web site and used it as a model for the Cullen family home. Like the Cullen house, Westlands is located well outside of Forks, along a river in a secluded spot. The centerpiece of the Westlands estate is a stately home built in the early 1900s now being restored. A classic misty, mountainous West End backdrop frames the home. The steady rolling sound of a nearby stretch of the Sol Duc River provides a soundtrack. On the property a section of old Highway 9 – the first paved road connecting Lake Crescent to Forks – now runs to nowhere, carried across a low concrete bridge coated in decades of moss. Stands of lime-green and yellow moss-coated trees point skyward along each side of the road. Unfortunately, the home was devastated by fire in March 2009 but homeowners John and Michelle Simpson have restored the home to its former grandeur.

The fine carpentry and interior design of their home is reflected in their nearby vacation rental cabins, The Cabins at Beaver Creek, which TripAdvisor.com rate excellent. Go to www.thecabinsatbeavercreek.com to make a reservation.

Photo courtesy Theresa Tetreau - Forks Library - North Olympic Library System
Forks Librarian Theresa Tetreau presents a Forks Library card to
Stephenie Meyer at the author's celebration day in Forks in July 2006.
The seed for the celebration was a call to Theresa made by the author
to organize a book signing at the Forks Library in the days when the
book series was beginning to take off across the country.

who was speaking at a gathering held in Meyer's honor at Tillicum
Park: "I would take exception to a few of the details but it's quite an
honor to have a nationally-known novel set in our community."

Forks Police Chief Mike Powell got into the role of Charlie
Swan, the father of Bella Swan, the main character in the Twilight
books. As Charlie Swan was noted as not being much of a cook, so
Powell gave Meyer a triple-decker, peanut butter-and-jelly sandwich.
The police chief also gladly offered to portray his fictional counterpart
in the film version of the book. A reading from Twilight was held
at the park, followed by a question and answer session by the author.
The party then moved downtown to the Forks Library where Meyer
autographed copies of Twilight for her local and visiting fans.

Today the signed books, some of them first editions, are rare col-
lectors items.

The author attended Sunday services at the Forks Latter-day
Saints church on Calawah Way with her husband and children, and
introduced herself to the congregation.

I first became aware of Stephenie Meyer's book Twilight early in 2006. A newspaper article in the Peninsula Daily News highlighted the young adult novel set in Forks with a cast of vampires as main characters. Little did I, or anyone else, anticipate that "Twilight" would mushroom into such a gigantic hit. In fact, after I initially ordered the book for the library, I really did not think much about the book again. It wasn't particularly the genre that I or my teenage daughters would normally be drawn to. It came as a surprise, then, when I received a phone call at the library from Stephenie Meyer. By late spring a number of positive reviews had been published about "Twilight" and sales were doing well, so I was thrilled that the author had taken the time to make a personal phone call to us. Ms. Meyer was looking for a place in the community where she could hold a book-signing event. Apparently, Forks High School student Nina Lau had contacted her previously and suggested the library as a potential site for a book signing. Together with Marcia Bingham and the other folks at the Forks Chamber of Commerce, we organized a book signing and author reading for July 20, 2006. Planning for the events was so much fun. When we finally met with the author, we found her to be warm and personable. I most admired how kind and open she was with her young fans. And what fans she has! It was so exciting

when nearly 200 young people and their families came to that first Forks book signing. The readers were thrilled to meet their favorite author and we librarians were tickled to see teenagers so enthusiastic about a book. We hope Ms. Meyer has a long career inspiring readers around the globe.

Twilight inscription from Stephenie Meyer's 2006 book signing in Forks, courtesy Janet Hughes, J.T.'s Sweet Stuffs.

Theresa Tetreau
Branch Manager
Forks Library

Meet <u>Twilight</u> author
Stephenie Meyer

BOOK SIGNING July 20

SCHEDULE OF EVENTS
5:00 PM Tillicum Park – Book Reading, Q & A with audience
6:00 PM Forks Library – Book Signing

Book available for purchase
at Fern Gallery in Forks and
at book signing

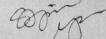

HOSTED BY
Friends of Forks Library
Forks Chamber of Commerce
North Olympic Library System, Forks Branch

Photos courtesy Forks Library - North Olympic Library System

Forks Police Chief Mike Powell's fried peanut butter and jelly sandwich he presented to Stephenie Meyer.

Traveling to Forks

Forks is the hometown of Twilight and the wettest town in the lower 48 states, with about 120 inches of rain each year. Twilight visitors experience the misty beauty of the rain forest atmosphere of Forks and the mysterious, dramatic Pacific Coast at LaPush. While enjoying their Twilight time in Forks, visitors also will find great day-hikes on the coast and in Olympic National Park, fine restaurants that feature locally-caught Pacific seafoods, a timber museum and a wealth of Twilight lore.

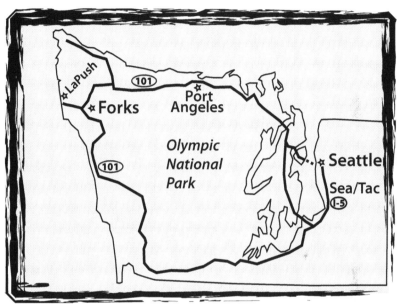

By air: SeaTac International Airport south of Seattle is the main jet airline hub for western Washington. It takes about four hours to drive to Forks from SeaTac, with the car ferry to Bainbridge Island or Bremerton short cuts. Kenmore Air in Port Angeles offers commuter flights to the Port Angeles airport with direct, daily scheduled connections from SeaTac (www.kenmoreair.com).

The Dungeness Line operated by Olympic Bus Lines offers two trips daily to and from SeaTac (www.olympicbuslines.com) to Port Angeles. Clallam Transit offers public bus service between Forks and Port Angeles, and Forks and LaPush (www.clallamtransit.com).

By car: From the south, Aberdeen, Wash. is about 100 miles south of Forks along Highway 101. The drive follows the coast, with fantastically beautiful Ruby Beach and the Kalaloch Lodge as good stops.

From the north, either head north into Seattle from SeaTac up the I-5 freeway and take the Bainbridge Island auto and passenger ferry from the Seattle waterfront, or if you want to save the cost of the ferry, take the I-5 freeway south and look for connections to the Tacoma Narrows Bridge. Once across the bridge follow state highways to Highway 101, which leads to the lavender fields of Sequim and then through historical Port Angeles (which is another Twilight location) along the Strait of Juan de Fuca.

Past Port Angeles, Highway 101 heads east for about 55 miles to Forks, meandering along the banks of pristine Lake Crescent, an alpine lake filled with emerald green water.

The west end of Lake Crescent marks the beginning of the West End of the Olympic Peninsula, the region where Forks is located.

Many Twilight fans make the trip south of Forks to the Olympic National Parks' Hoh Rain Forest interpretive center. About five miles off Highway 101 on the way to the park is a complex of shops, outdoor activities and a café. Gary and Charlotte Peterson run the Peak 6 Adventure Store here. Look for unique West End and Twilight items. This phone booth provides a clear picture of rain forest vegetation in the upper Hoh.

To the people of my favorite town —
I'm so honored that you've
chosen Bella's birthday, September 13th,
as Stephenie Meyer Day. Thank you
for being such gracious hosts for
my vampires!
You're wonderful!

A note from Stephenie Meyer to the people of Forks is at the Forks Chamber of Commerce's Visitor Information Center located just south of Forks across from the Forks Municipal Airport.

Forks Chamber of Commerce
and Twilight

Forks Chamber of Commerce Executive Director Marcia Bingham, Visitor Center Manager Mike Gurling, Visitor Greeter Merry Parker and Champber Promotions Director Lissy Andros are all familiar faces to the thousands of Twilight fans who visit Forks. Mike, aka "Mr. Twilight," was the first tour guide for the popular Twilight Tours of Forks and LaPush. The Forks Chamber originated the Stephenie Meyer Day - Bella's Birthday celebration held each September.

The Forks Chamber of Commerce's Twilight adventure began in the summer of August 2006 when a little-known author of a book set in Forks paid an official visit to the rural logging town.

Today the chamber's Visitor Center, located on South Forks Avenue a little ways south of downtown Forks, is the starting point for most Twilight visitors.

"She was charming, she was very happy to be here, pleased with the look of Forks, and I had a feeling we were at the precipice of something big," recalls Marcia Bingham, the executive director of the Forks Chamber of Commerce, looking back to the beginning of the Twilight phenomenon in Forks.

Marcia and Visitor Center Manager Mike Gurling help with orientations for Twilight fans prior to their roaming the town and the coast at LaPush.

"There were about 125 people gathered at Tillicum Park, from Canada, Oregon, California, Washington. I thought 'This is big,' but I didn't have an inkling that the book would become a national best-seller," she says of the 2006 event.

That weekend, Marcia says, Stephenie Meyer, a graduate of Brigham Young University in Provo, Utah, also attended the Sunday service at the Latter-day Saints Church in Forks.

"In the summer and fall of 2007 momentum was picking up; it was like something got shot out of a cannon, it mushroomed."

"We realized we needed to do something," Marcia said, "for the growing number of Twilight fans traveling hundreds, sometimes thousands, of miles to visit locations central to the books."

The concept for the annual gathering has mushroomed into a major event for Forks and for the world of Twilighters. Marcia said she and Mike considered using author Stephenie Meyer's birthday, but found

Forks' version of Bella Swan's 1953 red Chevy pickup (actually a 1952 Chevy) is the creation of Forks Councilman Bruce Guckenberg who found the vintage truck at West End Motors in Forks and painted it red with the help of other chamber members. Bruce is the manager of Sully's Drive In in Forks, and co-creator of Sully's famous Bella Burger. The Elwha River Casino donated the 1963 Chevy pick-up that is similar to the truck used in the film version of Twilight.

Marcia Bingham is all smiles while cutting the Twilight cake created by Forks Outfitters bakers. The cake was served at the Forks Library to cap off the day of Twilight festivities on Bella's Birthday, September 13, 2007. Mike Gurling of the Forks Chamber lends a hand.

out it fell on Christmas. Mike's encyclopedic knowledge of the Twilight book paid off when he mentioned that September 13 is Bella's birthday.

Marcia drove around Forks suggesting to local restaurants that they create themed-food items to help make fans feel welcomed. Her suggestion to Bruce Guckenberg, the manager of Sully's Drive-In, resulted in the best-selling Bella Burger, which Sully's serves with a free set of plastic vampire fangs.

Mike's Twilight book knowledge includes where Twilight locations in Forks and surrounding towns are located and how they related to places mentioned in the Twilight books. This provided the seed for the tens fo thousands of popular Twilight maps the Forks Chamber is distributing for free to fans.

"We developed a Twilight map, I did Twilight trivia tests – all to make people feel welcome," Mike recalls.

"The fans feel such high energy about Forks, and we didn't want people to blow them off," he says. "We began to get lots of compliments, we heard from fans that 'this is wonderful, you're embracing this so well.'"

Mike says unlike the Harry Potter books, which feature imaginary sites, the Twilight books are set in real locations in and around the town of Forks and on the coast at LaPush, the home of the Quileute Nation.

Still, "Some fans think Forks is a fictional place," Mike conjectures. "When they find out it's a real place, they come out here. A number of people have made this comparison to the Harry Potter books."

Marcia and Mike (along with Marcia's tiny, aging terrier Katie, whom she calls her "weredog") now are greeting thousands of Twilight fans each month.

They are still amazed when visitors arrive from across the Pacific, from England, Europe and other faraway places.

"One Australian girl dragged her family here; none had read the books, but she just had to come here," Mike remembers.

Another story they fondly tell is of the British grandparent who offered her teenage granddaughter a vacation wherever in the world she'd like to go – Universal Studios, Disneyland – instead the girl firmly declared she must go to Forks for "This is where Twilight happens."

A common reaction that still elicits a laugh at the chamber, even on days when the visitor center is wall-to-wall with Twilight fans, is the fan who comes in with a cell phone and starts looking around. She begins calling friends, "literally jumping off the floor," Mike says, screaming "I'm actually in Forks!"

"They are highly excited, almost bouncing off the walls, the excitement is so high; meanwhile we're grinning from ear to ear to see them so caught up in this fantasy," he says.

Mike's Twilight trivia quizzes are popular takeaways from the chamber's Twilight headquarters.

"As I read the books, I take notes; if something strikes me as an interesting tidbit, I note it," he says. "I try to limit the trivia list to 35 questions per book. I try to do a mixture of very easy questions with more obscure ones, such as what was the last name of Jasper in the 1800s before he became a vampire."

Mike receives requests from Twilight book clubs asking for copies of the trivia quiz. He also provides answer sheets via e-mail for fans who pick up quizzes during the Forks visits.

The top three fan requests for location information begin with Bella's House at no. 1, followed by the Cullen House and First Beach at LaPush, according to Mike.

"We discourage cliff diving at LaPush," Mike jokes. "If they want to be like Bella, who when she's feeling stressed hears Edward's voice in her head, they won't if they go cliff diving at LaPush, for the cliffs are sloped, they'll be bouncing off the slopes all the way down."

Mike's popular Twilight Tours of Forks and LaPush are given aboard the chamber's Forks Logging Tours van. The tours are limited by the capacity of the vans and Mike's time.

With the release of the first Twilight movie Marcia sees the Twilight boom continuing and growing in Forks.

"Even though the movie wasn't filmed here, it will feature Forks, and if sequels are filmed this could be a multiyear phenomenon," she said.

"Twilight has been an introduction to the rest of world to a beautiful area in the United States. It's been a reading incentive for millions," she adds.

The local economy is benefiting from the arrival of Twilight fans, and, Marcia says, this wave of visitors from an unexpected source is helping Forks and the West End of the Olympic Peninsula transition from the days when logging and fishing drove the economy to an era where tourism is added to that mix in a big way.

"We'll always be a timber town, but not to the same degree," she opines.

"There's the real world of Forks, and the fictional Forks, sometimes it's really the Twilight Zone," Marcia says.

"One guy called this summer," Marcia says. "I was going to come camping,' he said, 'but I understand you have a vampire problem.'"

"'Are you serious,' I said, 'No, we do not have a vampire problem.' He answered, 'What about the werewolves?'"

"Forks folks are receptive of the wave of fans arriving and Twilight is becoming more and more of an attraction in the town, Marcia concludes. "Things have evolved slowly – but we now have Twilight merchandise, Twilight-related food, more and more people are embracing it. Twilight fans are welcome here," Marcia says. "We want to show them a good time, and we want to share. We really try to make them feel welcome. We treat fictional characters as real people. We've had a lot of parents say, 'Thanks for making it fun for her.'"

A pictorial history of Forks by Larry Burtness and Chris Cook, culled from the collection of the Forks Timber Museum, is now available.

History of Forks

Forks is the main (and only) incorporated city in a region known as the West End of the North Olympic Peninsula. It is set near one of the few temperate rain forests in the world, and is considered the rainiest town in the continental United States with an average annual rainfall of more than 120 inches. The wet, misty rain forest climate is what drew author Stephenie Meyer to Forks when she searched on Google.com for a very rainy, isolated setting for her book Twilight.

Forks retains the spirit of small-town America, with friendliness and neighborliness a common trait of a town that proudly calls itself the "Logging Capital of the World."

Forks is the shopping, banking, law enforcement, education, medical and political center of the West End. The sole traffic light in Forks (and on the West End) is at the intersection of Division Street and Forks Avenue in downtown Forks. The traffic light is the only one along a stretch of two-lane U.S. Highway 101 running over 160 miles in length from Port Angeles to the north, and to Aberdeen to the south.

Two prison facilities – Clallam Bay Correction Center near the Strait of Juan de Fuca to the north, and Olympic Correction Center to the south beyond the Hoh River – are major employers for Forks residents.

The town was founded around a prairie burnt and cleared centuries ago by the Quileute Tribe from the dense forest to provide a feeding ground for deer and elk and other animals the tribe hunted. Forks is named for the nearby forks in the Bogachiel, Sol Duc and Calawah rivers. Some say the town first was named Fords after the family of Civil War veteran Luther Ford (and relative of automobile pioneer Henry Ford), one of the area's first settlers, who arrived in 1878, but the name was found to be in use. The town grew from its original farming community into a logging town over the decades thanks to the forests of gigantic first-growth Sitka spruce, hemlock, Douglas fir and red cedar trees that flourish in the rainy coastal environment.

Men of the families who later settled the area found work in the forest, in lumber mills and on the railroads that transported the huge logs to Port Angeles for shipping. The Rayonier locomotive on display at Tillicum Park in Forks is an artifact of that era.

The logging and milling industry flourished until the 1980s when a controversy over protecting the habitat of the Northern Spotted Owl caused the closure to logging of National Forest lands. Logging trucks were driven to the State Capital in Olympia in protest, and as unemployment rose, so did anger within the community over the environmental regulations. In the late 1970s, Hispanic immigrants began settling in Forks, earning a living by gathering salal and other plants for the nation's floral industry, plus, in season, edible mushrooms found at the base of the huge trees. Today the Hispanic community makes up about 20 percent of Forks' population.

Timber growing, felling and milling remain a major industry, with British Columbia-based Interfor's mills in operation at Beaver and the Forks Industrial Park north of town. Independently-operated cedar shake and shingle mills operate in and around Forks, with a number along Russell Road near the Forks Municipal Airport.

As logging waned in the 1990s, tourism picked up with visitors drawn by the spectacular scenic Pacific beaches and sea stacks; by the trails and pristine forests of the Olympic National Park (created in the late 1930s in part to protect interior and coastal stands of huge first-growth trees); and by river fishing for salmon and steelhead trout, ocean fishing for halibut and salmon, and deer and elk hunting.

Herds of Roosevelt elk freely roam the pastures of Forks.

Forks Fan Tour

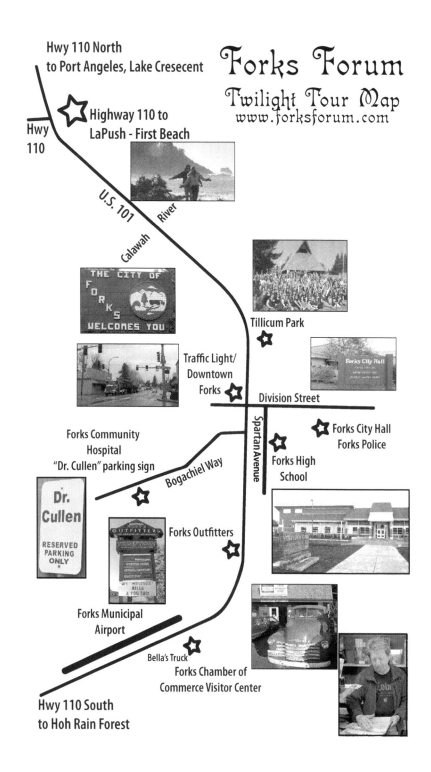

Hwy 110 North
to Port Angeles, Lake Cresecent

Forks Forum
Twilight Tour Map
www.forksforum.com

Highway 110 to
LaPush - First Beach

Hwy
110

U.S. 101

Calawah River

THE CITY OF FORKS
WELCOMES YOU

Tillicum Park

Traffic Light/
Downtown
Forks

Division Street

Forks City Hall

Forks Community
Hospital
"Dr. Cullen" parking sign

Spartan Avenue

Forks City Hall
Forks Police

Bogachiel Way

Forks High
School

Dr.
Cullen

RESERVED
PARKING
ONLY

OUTFITTERS

Forks Outfitters

Forks Municipal
Airport

Bella's Truck

Forks Chamber of
Commerce Visitor Center

Hwy 110 South
to Hoh Rain Forest

Forks Chamber begins taking visitors Twilighting

The original Twilight Tour van pulls up to Forks High School.

(Published in the *Forks Forum* May 2008)

See the homes of the stars!

Make that locations where vampires, werewolves and common West End folks live as mentioned in the best-selling Twilight books series and you have a van tour that outshines Hollywood excursions.

At least that's what the Forks Chamber of Commerce hopes as it launches its first Twilight tour on Saturday, June 7, 2008, at 9 a.m.

"I think mothers and daughters" will be fans of the tour, said Marcia Bingham, executive director of the Forks Chamber of Commerce, of the steady stream of Twilight fans who stop in at the chamber's visitor center located just south of downtown Forks. "We even just had interested grandparents, so it crosses the age span."

Bingham said on Friday a Twilight fan from Ohio had called to book a seat on the first tour. She said notice of the tour was first placed on the chamber Web site on Wednesday, May 14.

Tour driver, and retired Olympic National Park interpretive guide, Mike Gurling plans to take Twilight fans along the highways and byways of Forks and LaPush. Obvious stops include pointing out where Forks Police Chief Charlie Swan works at Forks City Hall, a ride down Spartan Avenue to see the classic brick facade of the old Forks High entrance where young lovers Bella and Edward go to school, and a spin to the coast to walk romantic sea-log-strewn First

Beach at LaPush, plus other accessible locales that inspired Twilight author Stephenie Meyer.

Gurling is the chamber's Forks Visitor Center manager and he is well versed in Twilight lore. Look on the chamber's Web site (www.forkswa.com) for photos of hundreds of Twilight fans who have arrived over the past months in small groups and as individuals. The chamber supplies them with Twilight packets that include a map of the West End with scenes from the book series well marked.

Gurling is a Twilight expert and knows the texts of the books in detail. He is the creator of Twilight trivia quizzes that are handed out to fans. Brief versions of his Twilight questions appear in the Table Topics folders that the Forks Forum and the chamber distribute to restaurants..

(*Editors note*: Two tour companies now provide Twilight tours of the Forks area. Twilight Tours in Forks is based on North Forks Ave. near Native to Twilight, and Team Forks Twilight Tours is based at Leppell's Flowers and Gifts-Twlight Central on South Spartan Ave. across the street from Forks Middle School.)

Fans place colorful push-pins, at least where there is still room, in this map located on the back wall at the Forks Chamber of Commerce's Visitor Information Center to mark their home town or homeland.

Bella Swan's House

Twilighters on tour make a stop at "Bella Swan's House."

A popular stop on the Twilight Tour is Forks' own version of Bella Swan's House, the fictional home of Forks Police Chief Charlie Swan that his daughter returns to live in.

The McIrvin family, the owners of the handsome craftsman-style home, graciously go along with the Twilight fantasy theme that has spread across Forks, however fans are asked to limit their tour to the residential street fronting their home.

On weekends especially, a steady stream of SUVs and cars, plus the occasional Twilight Tours visit, pull up in front of the family's driveway. Fans jump out, grab their digital cameras or cell phone cameras and snap away.

"I usually don't change my activity," Dave McIrvin, who is on the staff at Forks Middle School, says of the arrival of fans when he's working in the yard.

Dave enjoys chatting with the Twilight fans, standing in for Charlie Swan. However his wife, Kim, is the shy one in the family. "I tend to leave when the fans come," she says. "I'm not Charlie or Bella, I want it to be an authentic experience for the fans, unless I'm out gardening, then I say I'm Bellas gardener."

Dave and Kim say it's a coincidence that the front, upstairs bedroom is painted blue and has a window looking out on the street, and that their kitchen walls are yellow, just as described in the Twilight books.

"When we go out at night we leave the light on in the blue bedroom for the fans," Kim says. "That's the window that opens out, the window that Edward would come in; in the movie the window is much bigger."

The couple say notice of the similarity of their circa 1916 home to Meyer's description of the Swan home began to take off in late 2007. A request by Marcia Bingham of the Forks Chamber of Commerce to allow Twilight Tours to come by their house with the launch of the tours in June 2008 brought on the regular flow of fans.

The McIrvin family placed this sign in front of their home for Twilight visitors to photograph.

By the time of Forks' Bella's Birthday celebration in September 2008, the parade of fans out front became part of family life.

"We now have a warped sense of people coming by the house all the time and stopping out front," Dave says.

Their children are noticing the fans, too. Claire (the couples middle-school age daughter) made a couple of pans of brownies and sold them out front as Bella's brownies, Kim recalls.

Three-year-old Kathryn hears someone outside and simply says, "Oh, it's a Twilight fan, Twilighters."

Teenager Abby is having her own encounters with fans. "The idea of people driving by the window freaks her out a little bit," Kim says. "One night, late at night, she said, 'Mom someone is here in our driveway!' I said 'no,' but she said, 'Someone is here, I heard them pull up in the driveway.' So here I am looking out the door and I say see, there's no one here as I turn on the porch light. She said, 'Mom look!' and there was a bouquet of flowers on the porch with no name on it and she said 'See mom!...'"

The McIrvins feel the portrayal of Bella's house in the first Twilight movie is a bit off, and that their home is more akin to the author's description of the home in the books.

"You know, the thing is, if you read the books, Forks in the book is very true to Forks; except for the interstate, you can feel Forks," Dave says.

Kim, who has read and enjoys the Twilight books, says, "I

The view from inside Bella's house as touring Twilight fans stop by.

could see our house as Bella's house," and she can imagine Edward and his fellow Forks vampires out in the trees.

The McIrvins' version of Bella's house has been a magnet for visiting TV news crews and journalists who are happy to find a link to the book that also serves as a pretty image on screen and in print.

However, the McIrvins are holding off on allowing the curious newspeople and fans inside.

"Nobody can come inside until Oprah shows up," Kim says, expressing a dream of traveling to Chicago to be on the show herself.

The origin of the house is a story in itself. The craftsman home is said to have been built for the Warner family, who moved to Forks in 1916 to open the first automobile dealership in town. The home was located on South Forks Avenue, on the lot that today is home to the Almar Building. To make way for commercial development in downtown Forks, the house was moved to the corner of Russell Road and Highway 101 in the 1930s. In the late 1930s, work on widening Forks Avenue during the completion of looping Highway 101 around the Olympic Peninsula forced a move to a lot off of Russell Road. Then in 1990 the house was moved to its current location, on a quiet residential street.

Over the decades the home lost its luster, but it was restored to glory by Karen Hobbs, who purchased the building at auction for $148 in 1989. The McIrvins acquired the house in the fall of 1992, did some siding work on it and repainted and decorated the interior.

Cullen Family House

The picturesque Miller Tree Inn located on Division Street, just past Forks City Hall, Forks plays the role in Forks of Dr. Cullen and family's home. A white board hung near the front door of the inn provides frequent updates on the active social life of the Cullen Family. Inn keepers Bill & Susan Brager keep the notes up to date for Twilight fans who stop by. The Bragers note a remarkable coincidence regarding the inn's former owners. A Dr. Edwin Liebold once owned and resided in the handsome rural home. The doctor ran a family medical practice in a small office in downtown Forks plus attended patients at Forks' rural hospital. Dr. Liebold's family was noted to be about the size of the Cullen family, too. The Bragers welcome fans who love to snap photos of the home, but ask that the fans limit their sightseeing to the front yard.

Dr. Cullen's parking spot at Forks Community Hospital on Bogachiel Way is a popular stop on the Twilight tour of Forks. The sign has been relocated on the back wall of a clinic on 6th Avenue.

A wooden walkway with handrails built by the City of Forks at the city's welcome sign located at the north entrance to town in October 2008. City employees working on the sign are (from left) Keith Weekes, Dick Martin who is serving as foreman for the project and Jon Hart. Mayor Nedra Reed said the walkway will make it easy for parents of visiting Twilight fans to climb the grassy hill up to the sign for photos. Landscaping work also is planned at the site. The sign has become a landmark for visiting Twilight fans.

Forks High School
Home of the Spartans

Twilight fans gather at the entrance to the circa 1925 brick-front Forks High School Building for a Bella's Birthday tour of the school. The brick school building was demolished in 2011 to make way for a new, much needed Forks High School addition.

The students of Forks High School, and their identity as Spartans, are key elements of Stephenie Meyer's Twilight book series, and now in Summit Entertainment's Twilight movie series. Bella Swan and Edward Cullen, his brothers and sisters, are all Forks High students.

Comments in news reports and Web blogs are calling the school "the hippest high school" in the nation. Gear bearing the logo of Forks High – the Spartan – is selling both in Forks and across the Internet. Some of the clothing is authentic, most on the Internet appear to be knock-offs. Through a licensing agreement the student body is benefiting from sales of Spartan gear. Dollars are coming in to help fund student events at a time when education budgets are being cut back.

Forks students express a mixed opinion about all the attention their school – and themselves – are receiving.

As the Twilight phenomenon began to take off in 2006, the staff and students found it interesting and surprising when Twilight fans showed up to take photos of the brick facade of the school's now-shuttered brick building, and of the nearby wooden Spartan school sign. Now with the Twilight craze in full bloom, seeing the fans

Twilight film director Catherine Hardwicke shakes hands with then Forks High School Principal Kevin Rupprecht during a Forks scouting tour held in September 2007 for the film version of Twilight.

oogling their campus is common place.

There are Twilight fans within the student body – and likely tens of thousands of fans who would pay well to take their place in the classroom and halls for a day.

Forks High School Librarian Tammy Klebe, who is noted for her creative skills in creating wall-size library displays, decorated a wall of the school's library with a Twilight display.

Student body leaders worked hard and went all out to accommodate the overflow crowd that showed up to tour the brick-faced wing of the school on Stephenie Meyer Day 2008.

Tammy Klebe, Forks High School Library, contributed photo

Forks High School Librarian Tammy Klebe created this Twilight display she posted in the school's library in the old Forks High building.

Spartan varsity jackets used as film props

Varsity jackets owned by Spartan lettermen are highly visible in the Twilight movie. Star football running back Lucas (Luke) Dixon from the Class of 2009 rented his jacket to the film company and it appeared in the film in school scenes. "It was just an open thing, we heard over the loudspeaker that the Twilight movie was looking for jackets, 'if you want to rent yours bring it up to the office', they said," he recalls. "They kept it for about a month. A lot of people told me they saw the jacket in the movie, all said it was pretty cool." Of the fans traveling to Forks, Luke thinks, "It's pretty cool. You get to see a whole bunch of people come around. Forks is now more a commodity than just a place in the middle of nowhere that nobody knows about." Away from Forks, Spartan students and local residents are acquiring a high status due to their hometown's connection to the Twilight phenomenon. At a regional wrestling tournament, Luke says, fans were asking to take pictures of the Forks team. "One wrestler might have had his warm-up jacket stolen, because it had Forks on it," he says. "Most athletes think its kind of dumb. I've read all four books. I like them, they're a good series. My favorite character is Emmett, he's a big muscular guy that loves physical activities; that's pretty much me in a nutshell." Luke scored 29 touchdowns during the 2008 Spartan football season, which rated him third in the state in that category for all size schools. Luke graduated and is now attending college in Virginia.

Twilight fans take in a class at Forks High School during the Bella's Birthday school tour in 2008. Technology teacher Marty Dillon, playing the role of Mr. Mason, teaches a Twilight-based English lesson to lucky fans who are sitting in an actual school classroom.

This varnished wood sign located on Forks High School grounds on Spartan Avenue is a popular snapshot attraction for Twilight fans touring Forks. The sign is now located near the Quillayute Valley School District offices on South Spartan Ave., just down from Forks High School. Here Lexi Overstreet of Olympi Washington points to the sign during a Spring Break Twilight tour of Forks and LaPush.

Forks High School students split over 'Twilight' attention (2009)

By Cheryl Moore - Forks Forum intern, Forks High School student

Over the past few years the small town of Forks has become popular in the most unlikely of places. You could say that Twilight has affected our community and high school, but that could easily be taken too lightly.

Fans of all ages from around the world have read the books and may have even seen the movie, but the students of Forks High School are really the only ones who can fully understand the impact Twilight has had on this once little-known rural logging town.

Forks Forum interns Shyliah Justus (left) and Cheryl Moore report on Forks High School events for the Forks Forum.

Most students here realize how much Twilight has contributed to our community; some students who have read the books have gone beyond a fascination and have made short films about what Twilight would really be like in Forks.

"It's been fun," Principal Kevin Rupprecht remarked. He has been getting his hands wet trying to figure out what kinds of deals our school would be getting for licensing our Spartan trademark, and what the possibilities are for where this money could be going to. Mr. Rupprecht mentioned that the money could go towards scholarships, art programs, or just generally all to the ASB and they could choose what to use it for.

A book has been written by the studio producers of Twilight that is used as a fan guide for the movie. There are pictures included of Forks High School and local landmarks. A new book is currently being written by the director of the movie and he has asked Mr. Rupprecht for various pictures of our school, and even a photo of the two of them.

Mark Brandmire, FHS vice-principal, says he gets daily e-mails from fans all over wanting the real Spartan gear from the actual Forks High School. He said he gets acknowledged by random fans while wearing Spartan gear outside of city limits and he thinks that Twilight has been an "interesting phenomenon."

A handful of teens enjoy being involved with the Twilight events and wish for more. Bringing in business to the town's stores and attention to our school has helped make it a more enjoyable

Forks High School students Louie Ash-Kaufmann (left) and Dillon Elkins spot out-of-town Twilight fans roaming Forks Avenue at midnight during the August 2, 2008 Breaking Dawn festivities. The Forks High School students found the evening both amusing and perplexing as the usually quiet late night streets of Forks filled with out of town fans.

place to learn. The majority of students who were asked what they thought about Twilight were quick to say how much they liked the books.

On the other hand, there has been a controversy over Twilight among some FHS teens. A great deal of the students are not impressed with this series, and they feel that the notoriety brought by the books is ruining our town and bringing in too much unwanted attention. Students critical of Twilight are easy to spot, as are the Twilight supporters who help out tourists in local businesses and give tours of the high school.

Denise Gibbs, ASB Secretary, has contributed much to the Twilight events in Forks, such as giving FHS tours and selling Spartan gear to Twilighters during the Bella's birthday celebration. She has read Twilight, is now starting the second book, New Moon, and has watched the movie. She definitely liked the movie, but thought the book was better because not all scenes from the book were included. As far as raising money for the school, Denise thinks that Forks High School should never take advantage of the high demand for Twilight merchandise when planning fundraisers. The ASB already raises hundreds of dollars through donations from Spartan fans and sales of Spartan gear. The ASB has been trying to trademark the Spartan logo because sales of Spartan apparel could

Support Forks High School student activities - purchase Spartan wear directly from the high school

During school hours Monday-Friday during the school year Forks High School Spartan ware is available for sale at the front office in the administration building of Forks High School. Proceeds support the school's student activities. Pictured is the high school's official Spartan logo wear pinned up on a wall in the school office below a Twilight movie poster autographed by director Catherine Hardwicke for the school. Note the movie release date change.

be going to our school and benefiting the students. Businesses would still be allowed to use the Spartan logo if the trademark were issued, but would have to go through the Forks High School ASB. From a student's point of view, the trademark would be a great idea. The school could definitely use the extra money for repairs and beautifications.

As for the Twilight fans, students are very fortunate to have the opportunity to meet so many new people from all over the world. Forks' reputation is spreading globally because of the Twilight saga and, for the most part, the school has improved significantly in the years since the publication. Overall, Forks High School welcomes Twilight fans.

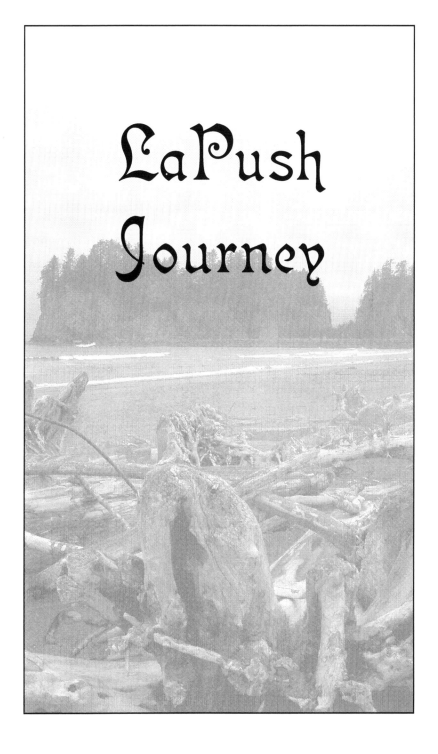

Quileute - People of the Wolf

"Thousands of winters before the arrival of the White Drifting-House people, the Quileute Indians and the ghosts of their ancestors lived and hunted here."

So begins the Quileute Tribe's official account of their people and homeland. "Quileute" is the preferred tribal name for their aboriginal lands, which once encompassed about 900 square miles, from the coast at LaPush north to Ozette, inland to the base of the Olympic Mountains and far to the south of LaPush. Today their homeland is a coastal area of one square mile commonly known as LaPush (the place name LaPush comes from the traders who once traveled the coast and derives from the French language-inspired Chinook trade jargon word "la bouche," or river mouth).

The Quileute are a Northwest tribe and known as a great seafaring people who traveled seagoing canoes sometimes as far as hundreds of miles. Traditionally, the Quileute lived in great cedar-plank houses near the ocean, wore cedarbark clothing, roasted salmon and other fish over fires, hunted whales and seals, and hunted Elk and other forest animals. The Quileute are known around the world as creating the most beautiful hand woven baskets and wood carvings. A notable event was a potlatch, where chiefs presided over great gift giving.

In the 1850s the Quileute Tribe were almost forced off the coastal lands they consider sacred, but refused to leave. A treaty signed with the United States in 1889 recognized the Quileute claim to the lands, and the Quileute Indian Reservation was then established.

In her Twilight books author Stephenie Meyer chose Quileute warriors as a counterpoint and rival to the Cullen vampire family, giving her Quileute characters – in particular Jacob Black – a werewolf identity.

Quileute elders ask that before visiting LaPush Twilight fans should be aware that Jacob and his werewolf clan are fictional, and their story as presented in Twilight is fictional.

Stephenie Meyer's Quileute creation story is also fictional, though roughly based on the Quileute's own account.

The Quileute account tells of a legendary being named K'wa'iti – the Trickster, the Transformer and The Changer – who created the first Quileute from wolves walking on First Beach who he turned into people, the first Quileute people.

As the young male Quileute Warriors in Meyer's books are tied closely to wolves through being werewolves who can transform themselves from human beings to wolves, so wolves were tied closely

Quileute Tribal School students spot whales off of First Beach at LaPush during the Quileute community's annual Welcome the Whale celebration held each year in early April. On this day Orcas, as well as migrating gray whales, were spotted along the coast. Author Stephenie Meyer based her fictional account of the Quileute traditions on information she read on the Internet about the Quileute people.

The whale greeting photo above was exhibited in the Seattle Art Museum at a special exhibit of Quileute artifacts and crafts that opened in 2010. Miss Ann Penn-Charles was among the dancers who performed at the exhibit opening. The exhibit opened at the Museum of the American Indian at the Smithsonian in Washington D.C. in early 2012

to a native Quileute society, the Tlokwali or Warrior Society who performed a Wolf Dance ritual. Author George Pettitt described the Tlokwali in his paper "The Quileute of La Push" published in the 1930s. Pettitt gathered information on traditional Quileute daily life and culture. He told of six-day-long Tlokwali initiation ceremonies held in winter.

This scenic view of First Beach is the first view of the coast at LaPush for visiting Twilight fans.

"Of all the initiations the most spectacular was the Wolf Dance Ritual of the Warrior Society or Tlokwali," Pettitt wrote. "It was held in a large ceremonial hall, entered by its members after going into the woods and howling like wolves. The leaders wore huge carved wolfhead masks."

In addition to the Tlokwail there were the Tsayeq, or Fishermen's Society; the Elk, or Hunters' Society; the Whale Hunters' Society; the Seal Hunters' Society; the Weather Forecasters' Society; and the Medicine Men's (or Shamans) Society.

You will hear Quileute words in the films, which highlights the importance of the Quileute language to the Quileute people and to linguists across the globe. The Quileute language is one of five known

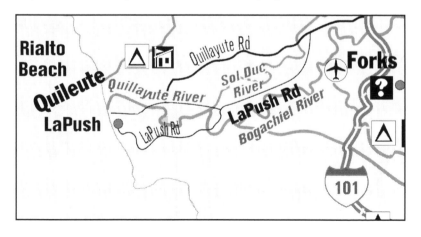

Chris Morganroth III preparing to tell Quileute legends at First Beach during the Bella's Birthday celebration held on September 13, 2008. Chris sent author Stephenie Meyer the elk skin drum he played (pictured below) during the Wolf Dance held at the Akalat Center at LaPush.

Drumming photo contributed by Beverly Laudon

languages that have no nasal sounds (no m or n) and is not known to be related to any other native or foreign language.

In the upcoming film version of "New Moon," the second book in the four-book Twilight series, the author focuses on Jacob and the Quileute people. In Twilight, the Quileute enter the scene, while they take center stage in New Moon. This connection was celebrated during the 2008 Bella's Birthday celebration by Quileute elder and storyteller Chris Morganroth III. Chris told of the connection between the orca (killer whale) and the wolf in Quileute traditions.

The Quileute's home is located about 20 minutes west of Forks on the Pacific Coast. The Northwest forest of the Olympic National Park runs to the east and south of the village, and the Quillayute River runs along LaPush's north end.

LaPush is about 14 miles from Forks. Turn off Highway 101 at State Route 110 – better known as LaPush Road. Once in LaPush you first pass the Lonesome Creek Store & RV Park. Supplies for

Photo contributed by Cathy Salazar

Twilight movie actors playing Quileute characters enjoyed a lesson in the Quileute language and were able to interact with young men from the Quileute Tribe in April 2008 in Portland. From left, Donovan Ward, the Twilight movie's Seth (Solomon Trimble) and Jacob (Taylor Lautner), Darryl Penn and James Salazar. "The people filming wanted the actors playing the Quileutes to talk with 'real' Quileute tribal members," Cathy Salazar recalls. Cathy is on staff at the Quileute Tribe's Department of Natural Resources. Cathy and Miss Ann Penn-Charles helped facilitate the meeting. "We spent about an hour or so visiting and sharing. They were very interested in the boys and hearing about the culture, what the boys do during their free time, what are things they really say, etc. This happened because Liz Sanchez is the aunt of Solomon (the actor playing Seth). Liz and Ms. Ann worked together to make the visit happen." Liz Sanchez is a teacher at Forks High School's Virtual High School. Liz sent an e-mail to the Forks Forum about her nephew: "Solomon Trimble is my nephew. I can tell you that Solomon as a boy came to visit up here (to Forks) and in college his plan was to become a teacher so he could teach at the Quileute Tribal School. Upon his graduation from college he did decide on law school though and was accepted, but then landed this role and chose to do this first and put law school off for now. He is a fine young man and we're so proud of him."

beachgoers and travelers is available here, and the LaPush Post Office is next door. Permits for camp fires on First Beach are available here.

A short distance along LaPush Road is the Oceanside Resort check-in building and gift shop. Past the Oceanside Resort the road makes a dog leg to the right and leads down to an intersection with Main Street. The River's Edge Restaurant is dead ahead, the Quileute Marina to the right. Take a left on Main Street to reach a free parking area that has access to First Beach and great views of the Quillayute River, First Beach, offshore sea stacks and the coast to the north. The Quileute Tribal School is on the hill to the southeast of the parking area.

Perhaps the top attraction for Twilight fans visiting LaPush are beach logs near the ball field at LaPush, just past the Oceanside Resort, and at other locations along First Beach. The logs are signed in charcoal by visiting fans.

The Quileute Oceanside Resort at LaPush offers visiting fans a comfortable and stylish stay in a growing number of oceanfront guest rooms. The resort is complimented with many ties to the Quileute people and their culture. Dozens of RV campsites are also available for rent, at two oceanside locations, both a short walk to First Beach. The resort dates back to the 1930s when the first visitor cabins were opened.

First Beach is a romantic setting for a Twilight walk at sunset with Ak•Ā•Lat (James) Island and sea stacks in the background, huge beach logs lining the shoreline and Pacific waves rolling in.

On the way to LaPush are two trailheads that lead to beaches located within the Olympic National Park. The names are simple – Second Beach and Third Beach. A moderate hike from a parking lot located on Quileute takes you to scenic Second Beach, a beach that has been named one of the most romantic in the United States. The parking lot is just up the road from the Lonesome Creek Store at LaPush where refreshments can be purchased.

One location you won't find is the sea diving cliff described by author Stephenie Meyer. The sea cliffs to the south of First Beach are a little too set back to provide a safe plunge into the ocean.

Read an interesting and informative description of the history of the Quileute people, listen to and learn words and phrases from the Quileute language, at the website www.quileutenation.org. Also please follow photography guidelines when on Quileute land, see their website for a detailed explanation.

The Quileute Tribe's Oceanside Resort check-in building at LaPush.
Twilight-themed gifts are sold at the gift shop located in the resort lobby.

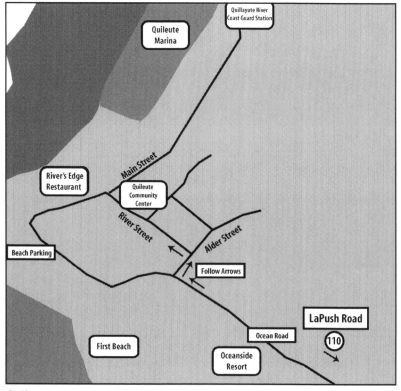

LaPush streets and Twilight-related sites.

LaPush 'Twilight' activities

• Walk First Beach at LaPush, or hike into Second Beach, a crescent black sand beach noted as one of the most romantic beaches in the United States.

• Drum with the Quileute community at the weekly Wednesday night Healing Circle drumming and pot luck held at the Quileute Community Center across from the Quileute Marina in LaPush. Visitors are welcomed and encouraged to attend.

• Enjoy a breakfast, lunch or dinner with a spectacular view of sea birds, seals, ocean and river vessels at the River's Edge restaurant adjacent to the Quileute Marina (open year-round).

• Stay at an oceanfront room at the Quileute Oceanside Resort.

• Shop for Quileute-made Twilight souvenirs at the Oceanside Resort visitor center and at the Lonesome Creek Store.

• Attend Quileute Days the third weekend in July, watch the colorful parade, have fun at the street fair, see the unique motorized canoe races, eat Quileute-style at a salmon bake.

• Join in the fun at Surfing & Traditions and watch longboard and shortboard surfers compete at First Beach in early July.

• See migrating gray whales in the spring and fall from a whale watching cruise or along First Beach.

• Go charter fishing or whale watching from the Quileute Marina.

• Help fund Christmas presents for needy children by bidding on unique Quileute crafts and a long list of other West End items at the Cherish Our Children auction held in early December at the Akalat Center.

• Buy smoked salmon from LaPush to take home.

• Mail a postcard with a LaPush postmark at the LaPush Post Office located next door to the Lonesome Creek Store.

Beach fire permits must be obtained at Lonesome Creek Store
Please do not remove stones, sand or wood from First Beach

Quileute-made crafts, logo clothing for Twilight fans available at Oceanside Resort

Naomi Jacobson creates these cedar bark bracelets and adds tiny wolves and crystals to them. Naomi may also be reached at quileutebellabracelets@yahoo.com.

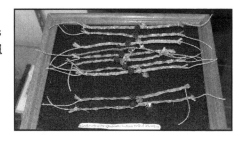

Cathy Salazar's Quileute baskets woven of cedar bark and other materials and featuring traditional Quileute designs such as the gray whale are available.

Quileute-themed hoodies and T-shirts feature Quileute wolf designs.

To shop online for official Quileute-made items look for the www.quileute-store.com link at www.QuileuteNation.org Web site.

Lonesome Creek Store - Bella's Bulletin Board

The Lonesome Creek Store & R.V. Park at LaPush serves at LaPush's general store. Supplies for a beach lunch, or quick snack, can be purchased here. On the facade of the building are reproductions of Quileute tribal masks and related animals, birds and marine mammals including the wolf. Fans are welcome to leave behind messages on Bella's Bulletin Board, which is located on the store's porch.

Second Beach

Second Beach south of LaPush at low tide. Author Stephenie Meyer implies that Bella Swan enjoys walking along the beautiful tide pools found at Second Beach. The hike to the beach is rated as a moderate one. Olympic National Park rules disallow removal of rocks from the beach.

Quileute Marina

The Quileute Marina at LaPush is a hub of recreational fishing and commercial fishing activities. Whale watching boat tours during warm weather whale migrations are being offered from the port.

Quileute Traditions

Quileute paddlers head out past Little James Island on their summer-time paddle journey to Lummi in 2007. During the summer of 1997, James Island or Ak•A•Lat was the site and symbol of the International Gathering at LaPush where 23 tribes paddled to celebrate the revival of their ocean-going canoe traditions.

Healing Circle drumming

Wednesday evenings at LaPush is the time for Healing Circle drumming and pot luck at the Quileute Community Center. Visitors are welcome to join in at this gathering. Here dancers circle the drum circle while community members look on.

A Quileute totem pole stands in front of the River's Edge restaurant. The restaurant is opened during warm weather and located at the Quileute Marina at LaPush, and offers spectacular views of James Island and sea birds in action along the Quillayute River.

Beverly Loudon of the Quileute Tribe joined in the fun at the 2008 Bella's Birthday celebration at Tillicum Park. Beverly is a member of "Team Jacob," she says. Beverly created the Twilight collage pictured above that tells of Twilight, First Beach and LaPush.

Twilight fans recall Bella's romantic beach scene at First Beach in LaPush by writing their names in charcoal on huge drift logs. A special, huge drift log (not the one pictured here) at First Beach near the Lonesome Creek Store is popularly known as "Jacob's Quileute Story Tree." Twilighters are asked to use only charcoal to write on the tree, using permanent markers or paint mars the log and shows disrespect for the Quileutes and a place they consider sacred.

Bella's Birthday Stephenie Meyer Day

Stephenie Meyer Day Celebration
September 10-12, 2010
Forks & LaPush

September 9, 2010
Special Section of
FORKS FORUM

Happy Birthday Bella!

Bella's Birthday 2007

Forks Forum staffers (from left) Janeen Howell, Traci Kettel and Mamie Morales hold their Twilight hunting permits in front of Forks High School during 2007 Bella's Birthday festivities.

(Announcement from the Forks Forum)

A day full of events honoring Stephenie Meyer, the author of the Forks-set national bestselling Twilight book series, is set for Forks on Thursday, Sept. 13. The date marks the birthday of Meyer's fictional Forks High School student Bella. Bella's romance with Edward, who is a teenage vampire and Forks High student, is at the heart of the book series. The day kicks off with the issuing of commemorative "hunting permits at the Forks Chamber of Commerce's Visitor Information Center at 1411 S. Forks Avenue. The permits map out Twilight locations in Forks and have boxes for rubber stamping.

Wax vampire teeth will be given out at JT's Sweet Stuffs, garlic cloves at J&P Produce and mini first aid kits at Chinook Pharmacy. At 10 a.m. Mayor Nedra Reed will read a proclamation marking the day as Stephenie Meyer Day in Forks. Photos of those coming dressed in costume as Edward and Bella will be taken at Forks Library at 4 p.m., and at 4:30 p.m. a birthday cake for Bella will be served.

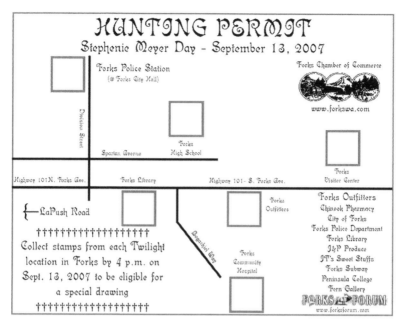

During the 2007 celebration fans collected stamps at locations that appear in the Twilight books with this Forks "hunting permit" created by the Forks Forum and the Forks Chamber of Commerce.

At the 2007 Bella's Birthday-Stephenie Meyer Day event Twilighters began arriving in Forks with messages marked on their car windows, wearing T-shirts showing affection for Edward Cullen and Jacob Black.

Bella's Birthday 2008

Twilight fans gather round the Tillicum Park Pavilion to choose the 2008 Bella's Birthday/Stephenie Meyer Day celebration Bella look-alike winner. Both local fans and visiting fans took part.

With dozens of digital cameras and cell phone cameras clicking away, Forks Mayor Nedra Reed reads a proclamation naming September 13, 2008 as Stephenie Meyer Day in the rural logging town. Tillicum Park in Forks served as the central staging area for the day

Schedule of Events - Bella's Birthday/Stephenie Meyer Day
Saturday, September 13, 2008

• 8 a.m. – Breakfast at Forks Congregational Church 280 South Spartan Ave. (directly across from Forks High School)

• 9 a.m. - Noon - Sign up for a drawing of four T-shirts "I was bitten by breaking dawn" and receive free stickers and buttons that the Forks Forum are giving away. 494 South Forks Avenue

• 10 a.m. – Tour of original circa 1925 brick Forks High School on Spartan Ave.

• 10 a.m. – Twilight items only sale booths open at Tillicum Park in Forks. (north end of town)

• 10 a.m. – Raffle Forks Avenue Real Estate 341 North Forks Avenue

• 10 a.m. – Cake Walk JT's Sweet Stuffs 80 North Forks Avenue

• 11 a.m. – Tour of original circa 1925 brick Forks High School on Spartan Ave.

• 11 a.m. – Drink blood red punch at the Forks Library book sale 171 South Forks Ave.

• Noon – Forks Mayor Nedra Reed reads Stephenie Meyer Day proclamation at Tillicum Park.

• 1 p.m. – Tour of original circa 1925 brick Forks High School on Spartan Ave.

• 1:30 p.m – Birthday cake for Bella served at Tillicum Park

• 2 p.m. – Join in the Bella's Birthday group photo shoot at Tillicum Park

• 2 p.m. – Read your favorite Twilight book series passage aloud at Tillicum Park

• 2:30 p.m. – Edward/ Bella/Jacob look alike contest judging at Tillicum Park with special prizes for winners.

• 3 p.m. – Open discussion on values represented in Twilight book series at Tillicum Park

• 6 p.m. – Wolf dance at Akalat Center in LaPush (about 20 minutes from Forks down LaPush Road (State Highway 110) on the left as you enter LaPush (there is an admission charge)

• 7 p.m. – Bonfire and storytelling at First Beach in LaPush (just down the hill towards the coast from the Akalat Center)

2008 Bella's Birthday - Tillicum Park - Group photo

Don Grafstrom, a Forks Realtor with Lunsford & Assocs., served as emcee for Twilight memorabilia raffle prize drawings. Here ecstatic Twilight fan Sarah Barnes of Silverdale, Wash. comes away with a Twilight movie poster donated and signed by Twilight film director Catherine Hardwicke.

Forks True Value Hardware owner Bob Stark stands with a special Twilight-decorated porta-potty placed in his parking lot in downtown Forks for the comfort of visiting fans other other Forks visitors.

Stephenie Meyer Day Committee

The Stephenie Meyer Day/Bella's Birthday Committee now heads up the annual celebration held in mid-September mostly in downtown Forks. Here the committee gathers in May 2012 to plan the 2012 celebration. Go to www.stepheniemeyerday.com for more information.

The Stephenie Meyer Day/Bella's Birthday programs are published by the Forks Forum. Online readable copies are located at www. forksforum.com/twilight

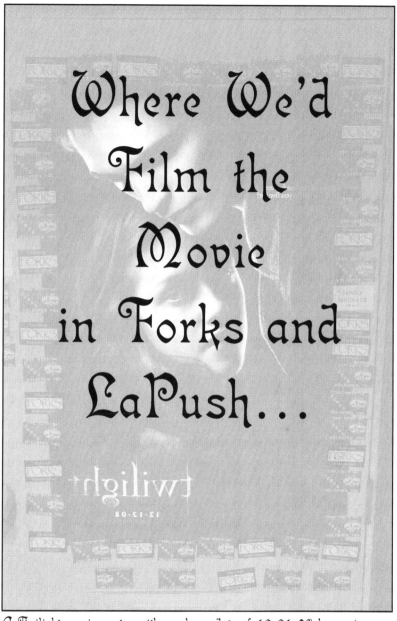

Where We'd Film the Movie in Forks and LaPush...

A Twilight movie poster with a release date of 12-21-08 hangs in reverse in the window of the Forks Chamber of Commerce's Visitor Information Center, and symbolizes the "other side of the looking glass" some Forks residents feel about Twilight being set in their town.

Forks Homes

"Cullen" is the name on the mail box at entrance to the Miller Tree Inn on Division Street. For Forks Twilight fans, the bed & breakfast inn portrays the home of the Cullen clan.

This restored craftsman-style home in Forks serves as a model for Bella Swan's home. The home is a private residence and visitors are welcomed to take photos, but not disturb the home's owners.

Westlands

This pasture, misty mountain and moss-covered tree backdrop captures the essence of a rural West End setting at the Westlands estate.

Forks High School

Forks High School's circa 1925 brick building is now demolished. This building was the ideal location for the school Bella Swan and Edward Cullen attend. A 21st century Forks High School buiding opened for students in January 2012.

Forks and LaPush were in the running as Twilight movie locations

Due to logistical and financial reasons, Summit Entertainment chose to film the first Twilight film at locations in Oregon and southern Washington. Twilight director Catherine Hardwicke scouted First Beach at LaPush in January 2008 and hoped to film at least one scene on the West End of the Olympic Peninsula, the region where author Stephenie Meyer choose to set Twilight.

The movie version of "New Moon," the second book in the Twilight series, is based in Vancouver British Columbia. However, film promotion efforts in Washington state are underway and aimed at attracting location filming for the final two films in the series.

"The new incentive legislation makes Washington state a much more compelling production destination," WashingtonFilmWorks Executive Director Amy Dee told the Forks Forum in April 2009. "Since the Governor signed the bill our office has been flooded with calls from filmmakers and production companies from around the world. That said, my first call after I got the news the bill had been signed was to Summit Entertainment to talk them about the Twilight sequels!"

(From the January 30, 2008 Forks Forum)

Local Twilight fans and businesses were disappointed in the choice, but have hopes that future films in the "Twilight" series will feature locations in and around Forks.

How the news that Twilight locations were chosen elsewhere

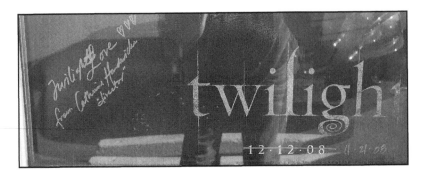

Twilight director Catherine Hardwicke loves Forks, and sent film promotion posters she autographed to the Forks Chamber of Commerce and to Forks High School.

LaPush

unfolded in the pages of the Forks Forum in early 2008.

Twilight film director Catherine Hardwicke scouted First Beach at LaPush on Quileute Tribe lands on Wednesday for location filming of scenes planned for the upcoming screen version of the best-selling Twilight book series.

During her scouting at LaPush, Hardwicke said Kristen Stewart, who plays Isabella Swan, the lead female role in the film, and other actors would travel from Portland to film scenes at First Beach. The story features a fictional member of the Quileute Tribe named Jacob Black who is a teenage werewolf in the story. The director said second-unit, background shot, filming of locations in Forks would also be done during the upcoming production of the teenage vampire love story.

Twilight film director Catherine Hardwicke poses on Jacob's Quileute Story Tree near Lonesome Creek at First Beach with James Island at LaPush in the background in January 2008.

Principal location filming is scheduled to begin in February in Portland. No dates for the LaPush filming were announced. Hardwicke said she would have loved to film mostly in Forks and other West End locations, but Oregon provided financial rebates to the film production company worth considerably more than those offered by Washington state.

Davis was behind the camera for Hardwicke's earlier hit films The Nativity Story and Lords of the Dogtown, and is a veteran cinematographer.

Hardwicke, Marshall, Davis and location director James Lin flew from Portland to the Quillayute Airport aboard a small prop plane on Wednesday morning for the location scouting tour. The Forks Chamber of Commerce provided their logging tour van to the filmmakers.

The Twilight film version is scheduled for release during the 2008 Christmas season.

LaPush surfing

Surfing at LaPush would provide a perfect backdrop for Twilight scenes at the Quileute Tribe's oceanfront homeland. Windy, blown-out surfing waves at an Oregon beach were used in the film version of Twilight.

Twilight filming at LaPush cancelled

(Forks Forum April 16, 2008)

LaPush is out as a location for filmmakers creating a movie version of the best-selling, Forks-set book Twilight.

A crew of eight surfers cast as extras in the film by a Portland casting company received word Thursday that the filming was off, Frank Crippen, owner of North by Northwest Surf Co. in Port Angeles said in a call to the Forks Forum.

The Forks Chamber of Commerce also reported cancellation of a block of 30 rooms reserved for the Twilight cast and crew at Pacific Inn in Forks.

The movie company was slated to arrive on the West End in late April to film a scene at First Beach in LaPush featuring Bella and Edward, the two lead characters in the film.

Twilight director Catherine Hardwicke flew up to the Quillayute Airport outside of Forks in late January in a small plane with the film's director of photography and location director. They walked off a scene where Bella and Edward walk atop a large fallen beach log near the mouth of Lonesome Creek.

Earlier, location scouts had toured Forks High School and took numerous photographs of the high school and its grounds.

Instead the Twilight production crew went with the brick-faced main building at Kalama High School in southwest Washington.

Principal filming is being done in Portland, with Kalama about 35 miles away. Reportedly, the beach scene is being filmed at Indian Point on the Oregon coast.

Reports from Port Angeles had teenage Twilight fans on the lookout for a film crew in the port city last week. However, the teens likely misread a report of Port Angeles filming on the Internet, with filming taking place at a substitute for Port Angeles at an Oregon or southwest Washington location.

During her January visit to LaPush, Hardwicke told the Forks Forum that Oregon was chosen for filming due to financial incentives from the State of Oregon. The director – who directed Lords of Dogtown, The Nativity Story and other feature films – said she would have used Forks if Washington state had offered similar support.

Forks fantasy movie locations

Forks - baseball meadow

This meadow located outside of Forks, near the boundary Forks vampire - LaPush werewolf boundary line, would have served well as the location for the Cullen family baseball game.

This sign used to hang on a rock wall near the meadow, placed by unnamed Twilighters.

Twilight filming underway in Kalama

(Forks Forum March 26, 2008)
The filming of the movie Twilight is underway in Kalama, about 35 miles north of Portland.

Kalama High was chosen for its close proximity to the principal filming locations in Portland, and because the brick front walls of the schools look like the front of Forks High School, though on a much larger

Kalama High School in Southwest Washington state served as a stand-in for Forks High School during the filming of "Twilight" in 2008.

scale. The fictional story of the international best-selling book is set in Forks.

Kalama High School students are posting short video clips on You-Tube.com and random digital photos of actors and location filming. Digital photos posted on the Internet show a prop Forks High School sign has been placed on the front of Kalama High School, and a Spartans booster poster hanging on the wall of the Kalama gym. Apparently, the stars of the film will be on the West End for only a few days of filming.

Casting call e-mails looking for experienced surfers are arriving in Forks, and give location shooting dates at LaPush somewhere within the time frame of April 23-25.

The student parking lot at Kalama High School is the site of key scenes in the film "Twilight."

A Kalama student posted this message on the twilightlexicon.com Web site on Tuesday, March 18: "Filming continues throughout the week at Kalama in their labs, gym, cafeteria and of all places believe it or not, their wrestling room. The hospital scene will be shot there later this week."

Forks Police Department

Former Forks Police Chief Mike Powell frequently served as a stand-in for Bella Swan's father, Forks Police Chief Charlie Swan, he would be perfect in the movie role. Actual Forks Police Department emblems are used in the Twilight movie.

Three Rivers

The border line between Quileute werewolf turf and Forks vampire territory is marked as the spot where Mora Road and LaPush Road meet at the Three Rivers store and restaurant. This sign the latest version.

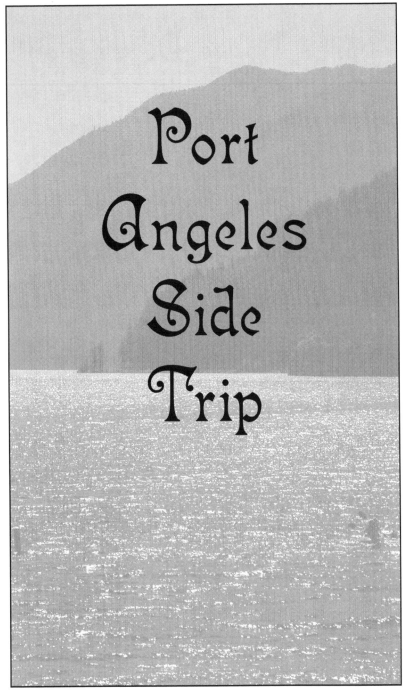

Port Angeles Side Trip

Scenic Lake Crescent, a memorable sight on the road to Forks.

Port Book and News in the historic downtown section of Port Angeles is considered by many Twilight fans as the bookstore Bella shops at in Twilight. The well-stocked, independent bookstore held a special midnight book release party for Stephenie Meyer's book Breaking Dawn in August 2008, and has a special Twilight shelf filled with Twilight books and interesting Twilight items.

Twilight fans often dine at the Bella Italia restaurant in Port Angeles, reliving Bella and Edward's romantic first date. Bella Italia is located at 118 East First Street in the downtown section of the city located along the Strait of Juan de Fuca.

The Necessities and Temptations gift shop is located within walking distance of the Victoria ferry in downtown Port Angeles. Robin Sheriff and Sarah Abbitt, and friend, stand in the gift shops' Twilight store-within-a-store. Owner Edna Petersen's popular shop is a must-see for Twilight fans visiting Port Angeles.

The proprietors of Miller Tree Inn in Forks set up a Cullen Christmas display with names of Twilight fans who have stayed at the inn.

Marcia Yanish (right) greets Twilight Christmastime visitors Lisa and Amber Rigsbee of Huntington Beach, California at the Forks Chamber of Commerce's Visitor Center.

Cullen Family Christmas stockings are hung from the mantle at the Miller Tree Inn in Forks.

The Cullen's Night Before Christmas, as adapted by Susan Brager, Innkeeper, Miller Tree Inn, Forks. (To read all the verses visit the Miller Tree Inn)

> T'was the night before Christmas and all through the house
> Not a Cullen was sleeping, except for one mouse.
> The stockings were hung by the chimney with care,
> But since vampires are sleepless, Santa had to beware.

Twilight snow fun: Katrina Zalewski of Brooksville, Florida (left) and her MySpace.com Twilight fan buddies Renee Sokoloff (center) and Shannon McCue from Eastern Washington and New Mexico drove up from Tacoma to take a Twilight tour during Christmas week 2008. Here the ladies brave the snow to get a photo in front of the Forks Chamber of Commerce's Bella truck. A steady stream of Twilight fans toured the town over the holidays despite the bad weather. The trio said the drive up through Port Angeles wasn't so bad.

The entrance to Forks covered in early winter snow. Pictured is the popular Forks welcome sign and a Forks Outfitters sign. The City of Forks has installed a ramp up to the sign for Twilight fans.

Twilight

Shop,

Dine,

Stay

Twilighters Krista Frenzel (left) and Janae Telford from Everett, Wa.

Forks Outfitters - Forks Thriftway
950 South Forks Ave. 374-6161
www.ForksOutfitters.com

Forks Outfitters is where Bella shops in the Twilight books, and the sporting goods department might be where she worked. A large selection of unique Twilight and Forks themed clothing is available. You'll find Twilight books specially marked as bought in Forks. Look for the store's Twilight-theme rain boots, a popular gift to take home from rainy Forks, Forks Outfitters is the grocery store of Forks, and features a deli, and a bakery where Twilight cakes can be custom ordered.

Leppell's Flowers and Gifts - Twilight Central
130 South Spartan Ave. 374-6931
www.forkstwilightcentral.com - twilightinforks@centurytel.net

Charlene Leppell Cross (center) creates and designs many of the shop's Twilight items. Look for Charlene in the popular "Twilight In Forks" DVD. Twilight flower arraignments from her shop are popular with visiting fans. Full-featured Twilight wedding ceremonies are available too.

Leppell's Flowers and Gifts is a long-time Forks business that features a variety of Twilight items that capture the charm of the rural logging town. Look for unique Twilight items created in-house by Leppell's plus Forks High School Spartan items, Twilight scrapbooks and original scrapbooking materials, Forks-Twilight T-shirts, and dozens of other Twilight keepsakes. Twilight flower arrangements are a speciality. The shop is located on Spartan Avenue, one block off of Highway 101.

The front door of Chinook Pharmacy features Forks' Twilight art work. Inside look for the special Twilight section.

Chinook Pharmacy's Pura Carlson designs unique Twilight and Forks shirts for the store, including the Forks-themed shirt above and one that ties Forks' famous rainfall to Twilight character Edward Cullen.

Native To Twilight 10 North Forks Ave. 374-2111
www.nativetotwilight.com

Native to Twilight owner Anna Matsche carefully selects choice coastal tribal art and gift items with Twilight and West End selections. Her selection seems to be ever expanding in her spacious store located in the heart of downtown Forks.

JT's Sweet Stuffs 80 North Forks Ave. 374-6111

Twilight memorabilia display case and selection of Twilight gifts. Meeting room available for Twilight event gatherings. A sweet shop, coffee shop, restaurant and ice cream parlor.

JT's Janet Hughes with her Twilight memorabilia display.

Twilight author Stephenie Meyer enjoyed the sweets at JT's during her early visits to Forks.
Look for her quote in JT's window.

The highlight of JT's Sweet Stuffs' special Twilight display case is an early copy of Twilight autographed by Stephenie Meyer during her 2006 visit to Forks.

Old Mill Trading Post - Located within 110 Business Park on LaPush Road - State Highway 110 - 374-3199

Along with this case of Twilight items, the Old Mill Trading Post offers western antiques, well-chosen gift items, children's toys, tribal items including hard-to-find drum making supplies and much more. Set aside time when you stop here to shop, there's much to see.

z3universe.blogspot.com

Bonnie Dunker of www.z3universe. com designs and produces Twilight and Forks bookmarks, magnets, buttons and more. Look for her in warm weather on Saturday at the Forks Open Aire Market.

Olympic Graphic Arts 640 South Forks Ave. 374-6020
olympicgrahic@centurytel.com

Full-color photo journal book and a local calendar featuring local Twilight sites and photos by Rico Menke. Digital color copies, graphic arts supplies.

Salmonberry - 120 S. Forks Ave. - 374-5500

This West End artisans gallery is located in downtown Forks. Look for the "Twilight Corner," which features quality Twilight items handmade in the Forks region. Featured Twilight artisans include Tena Gagnon's The Forks Forest items.

Alice's Closet - 130 S. Forks Ave. - 640-9646

Unique fine Twilight-themed clothing and jewelery selected and created by shop owner Staci Chastain. Alice's Closet is located in a shop located next door to the Salmonberry Gallery. Staci's goods have been a hit at Twilight Con gatherings. Check her Alice's Closet Facebook page for updates on the annual Stephenie Meyer Day celebration held in Forks in mid-September.

West End Surf 71 S. Division Street Forks 374-5251

Forks surfing T-shirts, skateboards, surfboards

Twilight van tours

Perhaps the most visible sign of Twilight tourism in Forks is the appearance on local streets of the town's two Twilight tour vans. The black Twilight tour van is operated by Twilight Tours In Forks, and the white tour bus is run by TeamForks Twilight Tours.

Both tours start out in Forks, tour the Twilight sites in town then head out to the coast for a look at LaPush, the Quillayute Prairie, the Three Rivers/Mora area and more.

Twilight Tours in Forks - www.twilighttoursinforks.com
374-8687 - 640-8709

Twilight Tours in Forks owner Travis Belles provides a knowledgable, fun tour of Forks' Twilight sites. Travis is a former Hollywood stars home tour guide, and is now a resident expert guide in Forks. Tours depart near traffic light on Forks Ave.

Team Forks Twilight Tours - www.teamforks.com
374-2123 - 374-6931

Team Forks Twilight Tours are led by Randy Bennett and departs from Twilight Central/Leppell's Flowers & Gifts. Randy is known for his fun, friendly, insightful tours of all the Forks Twilight sites.

Dining

220 North Forks Avenue
360-374-5075

Stop in for the "Bella Burger" - meat patty topped with Swiss cheese, lettuce, tomato and pineapple - with a special sauce, plus a free set of vampire teeth. Look for Sully's Twilight caps and T-shirts!

Shop where Bella shops and works in the Twilight books! All your grocery, picnic, deli, snack needs plus Twilight coffee and treats. Twilight clothing, books, DVDs and souvenirs. Look for Northwest food specialties. Full-service coffee bar, instant digital photo finishing.

www.forksoutfitters.com

241 S. Forks Avenue • Forks, WA 98331 • (360) 374-6769

Fun, Family Eating. Located on Highway 101 in the heart of Forks. Try the "Twilight Burger" and other tasteful "Bella" specials. Don't forget to try Jacob's blackberry cobbler as featured in the Twilight film!
www.forkscoffeeshop.com

Italian & American Specialties Dine In, Delivery or Take Out. Located on Highway 101 next to Forks Outfitters. Twilight specials include Bellasagna served with Edbread and Swan salad. New entrees honor Jacob Black and Bella. Menu is online at www.forksforum.com/pacificpizza.

"The Sweetest Place in Forks!" Located in downtown Forks serving sandwiches and soups daily. Hand-dipped ice cream. Twilight delights – chocolates made in Forks.

Located in the Evergreen 76 Gas station and mini mart on Highway 101 North Forks. Try "The Twilight Sandwich" a 6 inch or footlong sub with roasted chicken, ham, bacon and marinara sauce. Look for Twilight souvenirs and gifts too.

River's Edge in LaPush

The River's Edge restaurant is open from mid-spring into mid-fall and is located on the waterfront adjacent to the Quileute Marina. Diners are treated to spectacular views of James Ilsand, the Quileute estuary plus sea birds and harbor seals in action along the Quillayute River. Breakfast, lunch and diner is served. Call 374-5777

Vampire Warning!

The folks at the River's Edge restaurant created this vampire-in-cheek Vamire Threat Level sign. The sign is a take-off on the forest fire warning signs commonly found along highways in the West End. Joke Twilight T-shirts produced for local residents include one with a logger grasping a vampire by the neck.

Twilight-themed Accommodations

Pacific Inn Motel - 352 South Forks Ave. 374-9400
PacificInnMotel.com

Step into the world of Twilight. We provide an experience, not just a place to stay...
Stay in a Twilight-themed room...
• Includes a Forks area map highlighting all locations listed in the Twilight books
• Twilight Trivia
• Twilight dessert or burger gift

Dew Drop Inn - 100 Fernhill Road Forks 374-4055
DewDropInnMotel.com - (888) 433-9376

Features a brand new Bella Suite - Twilight-themed room. Look for the Dew Drop Inn's Facebook page for a thorough look at their Twilight rooms and Twilight theme tie-ins.

Miller Tree Inn - 654 East Division St. 374-6806
MillerTreeInn.com

Forks' "Cullen Family Home"

We invite you to come and share our beautiful 1916 farmhouse, located on the edge of town and bordered by trees and pasture lands in Forks. We offer a warm welcome, hearty breakfasts, spacious common areas, and quiet, comfortable rooms for a reasonable price.

Quileute Oceanside Resort at 320 Ocean Drive, LaPush (800) 487-1267 or (360) 374-5267 quileutenation.org.

Two RV parking/camping areas are available with hookups at LaPush.

Misty Valley Inn - 2 miles north of Forks on Highway 101 (877) 374-9389 mistyvalleyinn.com

Forks Motel - 351. South Forks Ave. - Forks (800) 544-3416 or (360) 374-6243 www.forksmotel.com

Olympic Suites Inn - 800 Olympic Drive - North end of Forks (800) 262-3433 or (360) 374-5400 www.olympicsuitesinn.com

Three Rivers Resort - 7764 LaPush Rd. (360) 374-5300 - www.forks-web.com/threerivers

Shadynook Cottages - 81 Ash Ave. - Forks (360) 374-5497 shadynookcottage.com

The Pacific Inn in Forks decorated its Forks Avenue window Twilight style. Forks-based artist Vern Kestand (bmwoodworx.com) painted the window.

Forks Forum & "New Moon"

Forks Forum Editor Chris Cook provided dozens of location photos to the producers of the Twilight film "New Moon" to be used in dressing locations filmed as Forks and LaPush in British Columbia. In turn, the film company sent the Forks Forum personally autographed photos of the film's three stars. The signed photos were donated to the Quillayute Valley School District's annual scholarship auction to raise funds to provide financial aid to local students.

"Twilight in Forks" DVD

Seattle-based film-makers producer York Baur (left) and director Jason Brown provided the world with a close look at "Twilight in Forks" through their successful DVD.

Twilight Territory - A Fan's Guide to Forks & LaPush 87

Acknowledgements

The Forks Chamber of Commerce's Twilight crew who have served as extraordinary greeters for the daily parade of Twilighters: Marcia Bingham, Mike Gurling, Lissy Andros, Merry Parker, Marcia Yanish, Judge Erik Rohrer. City of Forks Mayor Bryon Monohon, Attorney/Planner Rod Fleck, Dick Martin and crew, and the Forks City Council. At LaPush, the Quileute Tribal Council, Publicist Jackie Jacobs, Quileute elders Russell Woodruff and Chris Morganroth III; Vince and Sharon Penn; Miss Ann Penn Charles, Cathy Salazar and Beverly Loudon. Diane Schostak at the Olympic Peninsula Visitors Bureau. At Forks High School, Principal Rex Weltz, QVSD Superintendent Diana Reaume, Marty Dillon, Brenda King, Tammy Klebe, the Spartans and Lady Spartans, our interns Cheryl Moore and Shyliah Justus, Louie and Dillon. Bert Paul, Bruce Paul, Dave and Brenda Gedlund, at Forks Outfitters. Charlene Cross and crew at Leppell's Gifts & Flowers. The Stephenie Meyer Day committee. The crew at the *Sequim Gazette* for supporting the creation of this book. Forks Library's Theresa Tetreau and staff, and North Olympic Library System Director Paula Barnes. Bruce Guckenberg and family at Sully's Drive In. Rianilee and Travis Belles at Twilight Tours in Forks. Don Grafstrom. Carrol Lunsford and staff. Mark & Pat Soderlind, The Petersons and the Carlsons and staff at Chinook Pharmacy. Anna Matsche at Native to Twilight. Darren and Leah Grenno, and Nui, at West End Surf. Bill and Susan Brager at Miller Tree Inn. Forks Community Hospital's Camille Scott and staff. Biff Lesure at Junkyard Dog. Gary and Charlotte Peterson at Peak 6. Port Book & News, Edna Peterson at Necessities and Temptaions. The McIrvins, the Dixons, the Bowers, the Simpsons, the Hestands. The Shaw family and the Ray family. Mike Harmon and Carol Young, and friends, at Oil City Road and the Upper Hoh. The ladies at twilightlexicon.com and the thousands of Twilighters who have made their pilgrimage to Forks. Catherine Hardwicke. The Cullens, Blacks and Swans. Last but not least – Evelyn, Davy (LaPush shortboarder) and Christian (…they were riding down the road to LaPush!).

And especially to Stephenie Meyer whose dream launched all this.

To order additional copies of Twilight Territory go to www. forksforum.com/twilight, stop by the Forks Forum at 494 S. Forks Ave. in Forks or call (360) 374-3311

Your best source of Forks Twilight news, photos and Twilight tour information
Published weekly in Forks Washington

For the latest Twilight news from Forks go online to www.ForksForum.com

Made in the USA
Charleston, SC
18 September 2012